1 Introduction

At the 2017 Berkshire Hathaway shareholder meeting, the legendary investor Warren Buffett admitted that he missed the boat on investing in two of today's most successful tech companies: Google and Amazon. Buffett said he should have known early on that Google was going places. He remembered that Berkshire subsidiary Geico was paying $10 or $11 to Google every time someone clicked on an ad.

At the same time, Google has been consistently ranked as one of the best employers in the world. As of 2017, Google has been on Fortune's 100 Best Place to Work list for 11 years. For the sixth year running, Google has landed the top spot. According to LinkedIn, Google is the most sought-after place to work across the world.

Since 2011, Google has been offering above the market rate compensation package. In Google's early days, it didn't pay above market rate salaries. But, early-employees became rich because of Google's IPO and its stock appreciation. In January 2011 Google gave all employees an additional raise equivalent to 1X the employee's target bonus for the year. Google takes good care of its employees. Google's benefit package is one of the best in the world. Some of these benefits are unheard of in Corporate America. Just to give you a few examples of Google's excellent benefits:

- Free gourmet food and snacks. Unlike the junk food you see in typical tech companies, if you visit Google's cafeterias, you'll see fresh, organic, nutritious food.
- Employees can give each other "message credits" for a job well done on projects. The credit can then be redeemed for a free one-hour massage on campus.
- New mom can take 18 weeks of maternity leave and new dad receives 6 weeks of paid leave. Employees' stock continues to vest while they are on leave.
- If a Google employee passes away, all their stock vests immediately. In addition to life insurance payment, the employee's surviving spouse get half of the Google employee's salary for the next 10 years. Each kid will get $1,000 per month benefit.
- The 20% rule that allows Google employees to work on passion projects.
- And many other benefits.

Google has one of the best corporate cultures on the planet. It is non-hierarchical, believes in the good of people, and gives people a lot of freedom to create and innovate. It treats employees with respect and generosity.

Google has recruited and hired the most impressive array of talents in the technology industry. Just to give you a few examples of world class talents who are working at Google as of 2017.

- Vint Cerf: VP and Chief Internet Evangelist for Google. Recognized as one of "the fathers of Internet"
- Hal Varian: Chief Economist at Google, leading economist and founding Dean of UC Berkeley School of Information. When I was an undergraduate student at UC Berkeley almost two decades ago, I had the opportunity to interact with Professor Varian. He is amazing.
- Diane Greene: Co-Founder and former CEO of VMWare
- Dick Lyon: Inventor of Optical Mouse
- Andy Conrad: Geneticist who co-founded Genetics Institute (NGI). He served as its Chief Scientist and helped grow it into one of the largest genetics laboratories in the world.

Google continues to innovate and stay at the forefront of key technology trends such as cloud computing, machine learning, artificial intelligence, self-driving car, computer vision, etc.

In summary, Google has a great culture and an employee-friendly work environment. You'll interact with very smart people. You'll work on cutting edge technology and applications while learning a ton. And you'll get paid well with excellent benefits. It almost sounds too good to be true. Who wouldn't anyone want to work for Google!

No wonder Google receives more than two million applications every year. Google only hires several thousand per year, making Google 20+ times more selective than Harvard, Yale or Princeton. For example, Google hires about 0.25% of job applicants, while Harvard's admission rate was 5.2% in 2017. But please do not be intimidated by these numbers. It's much easier to apply for a job at Google by submitting your resume while college application process is much more involved and time consuming. So, Google has a lot more applicants each year (1-3 million) than the number of applicants at Harvard.

Google's hiring bar is high and the process is competitive, but there are ways for you to prepare for Google interviews that will significantly increase your chance to land an offer at Google. This starts with having a deep and accurate understanding of Google's business model, unique corporate culture and hiring practices. This guide goes behind the scene to reveal how exactly recruiting works inside Google. Combined with our coaching experiences of helping applicants to land offers at Google, we'll provide you a comprehensive framework to navigate the entire interview process at Google:

- How to find Google job lead. There is one method that is particularly important to Google.
- How to prepare for your first phone/Google Hangout Interview. Google's first interview is very different from other companies.
- How to prepare for your onsite interview.
- Who will make the hiring decision and how the decision will be made. What does this mean to you as you navigate the whole process.
- How to emulate Google employees to increase your chance to land an offer.
- Sample interviews questions and tips

2 What makes Google hiring process unique?

Please keep the following in mind as you navigate this process.

- Google invests heavily upfront in recruiting to make sure they hire the best people who fit Google's culture.
- Google hires slowly and methodically. Sometimes it is almost too slow for candidates.
- Google applies tons of data analytics in the hiring process.
- Google has a unique process to review and approve hiring decisions.
- Google's hiring philosophy focus more on "smart generalist" instead of domain experts (with some exceptions).
- Google's hiring approach has evolved over the years based on feedback from data analytics and learnings.

Alphabet vs. Google

In April 2014, Google's management team created a new entity called Alphabet, which essentially serves as a holding company to Google and other more speculative ventures. Google's cofounders, Larry Page and Sergey Brin, have long been fans of Warren Buffett, Charlie Munger and their holding company Berkshire Hathaway. As Google becomes a more mature company with a large amount of cash on hand, Larry and Sergey essentially created their own version of Berkshire Hathaway by establishing Alphabet the holding company.

Google still accounts for most of Alphabet's revenue and profit. But, it's important for any job applicant to have a basic understanding of Alphabet the parent company to Google, its core business (i.e. Google) vs. other innovative but early stage ventures, and future directions.

As of end of 2016, Alphabet has been in operation for 21 months. According to Larry Page, "Alphabet is about businesses prospering through strong leaders and independence."

Most readers of this book are probably applying for jobs at Google. But, it's important to note that Alphabet's job openings are not limited to Google. Alphabet operates a portfolio of companies and projects. Below is a list of exciting new Alphabet projects that might interest you as well. Most of these projects are independent entities/companies that roll up to Alphabet.

Category	Company Name	Notable Project/Products	Leader
Self-Driving Car	Waymo	Formed a partnership with Fiat Chrysler around their new plug-in hybrid Pacifica minivan	John Krafcik
Life Science	Verily Life Sciences	Debug project, which aims to stop mosquitoes in their tracks	Andy Conrad
IoT	Nest	Indoor and outdoor cameras, learning thermostats, and smoke alarm	Marwan Fawaz
Infrastructure	Google Fiber	Named fastest 2017 Internet Service Provider in the U.S. by PC Mag.	Greg McCray resigned in July 2017. Currently search for replacement.
Anti-Aging	Calico	Its mission is to build Bell Labs of aging research.	Art Levinson
Investment	GV	Venture Capital Arm of Google. $2.4 billion under management and more than 300 portfolio companies, including Nest, Uber, Slack and Flatiron Health.	David Krane
	Google Capital	Growth equity investment fund. Portfolio companies include Glassdoor, Thumbtack, Guesto.	David Lawee

| Drone | X (Alphabet's moonshot factory) | Wing – Drone Delivery | Astro Teller |

Google has a good track record of picking important projects long before others. The YouTube acquisition and the Android acquisitions are two good examples. Not only Google made the right acquisitions, it also has done a good job to grow these two businesses. Google has also been early in machine learning and artificial intelligence. Google Brain and Deep Mind are two examples in the machine learning/AI space.

Google is big on machine learning. It has the foresights to invest in machine learning related Research and Development. It started early, and it has already incorporated machine learning into many of its product and services offerings. For example:

- Use voice to search for information
- Google Translate
- YouTube recommendation
- Search for people and events that are important to you in Google Photo
- Improving energy efficiency of data center
- Helping self-driving cars to better detect and react to others on the road

In one aspect Google's cofounders are remarkably like Jeff Bezos of Amazon. As Larry and Sergey wrote in the original founders' letter, "Google is not a conventional company. We do not intend to become one." They have also said that they would "make smaller bets in areas that might seem very speculative or even strange when compared to our current businesses."

Similarly, Jeff Bezos had instilled a culture of "bold bets" and experimentation at Amazon. When I started working at Amazon in 2004, during my first company all-hand meeting, Jeff Bezos said that he was willing to make 3 bold bets each year. The 3 bold bets at that time were Amazon Web Service (AWS), Amazon Kindle, and a9 search engine. A lot of people were skeptical of the bold bets but two out of three bold bets have become multi-billion dollars businesses.

How much revenue does Alphabet makes in a year? How much of it comes from Google?

In 2016, Google's total revenue was $90.3 billion dollars. $89.5 billion came from Google, while the other $0.8 billion came from "Other Bet" category. (Alphabet groups non-Google revenue source under "Other Bet" category). As of end of 2016, Google accounted for 99.11% of Alphabet's revenue. "Other Bet" accounted for only 0.89% of Alphabet's total revenue.

So, Google revenue represents the absolute majority of Alphabet revenue. However, I would not dismiss the potential of the "Other Bet". Alphabet seems to be taking a chapter from Jeff Bezos' playbook. I wouldn't be surprised that in the future multiple billion-dollar businesses come out of "Other Bet".

What is Alphabet's cost of revenue? Where does the cost come from?

Cost of revenue in 2016 was $35.1 Billion, which is 38.87% of total revenue. So, for every $100 revenue Alphabet generates, it cost them $38.87 dollars. The single biggest cost was traffic acquisition cost of $16.8 billion, which was 47.86% of the total cost of revenue. So, Alphabet spent a lot of money on acquiring traffic and it represented almost half of its total cost of revenue in 2016. What exactly is traffic acquisition cost? We'll cover it later in this book.

How profitable is Google's bottom line?

Google is a cash cow. In 2016 Alphabet's net income was $19.5 billion, which was 21.59% of total revenue. It has operating cash flow of $36 billion. That's a massive war chest of cash!

Just to provide some context. The table below compares Amazon vs. Google in key financial metrics.

	Alphabet	Amazon
2016 Revenue	$90.3 billion	$135.99 billion
2016 Revenue Growth Rate	20%	27.08%
2016 Cost of Revenue	$35.1 billion	$88.27 billion

2016 Cost of Revenue/Revenue	38.87%	64.91%
2016 Net Income	$19.5 billion	$2.37 billion
2016 Net Income / Revenue	21.59%	1.74%
2016 Operating Cash Flow	$36 billion	$16.44 billion

A big portion of Amazon business is ecommerce/retail with very low margins. It is reflected in Amazon's lower profitability metrics (e.g. Cost of Revenue %, and Net Income %). Still, when you compare Amazon and Alphabet, it amazes me how much more Net Income and Cash Flow Alphabet generates. No wonder Warren Buffett recently said that not buying Google is Berkshire Hathaway's biggest mistake.

If Google accounts for most of Alphabet's revenue, where does Google's revenue come from?

They come from online advertising. Google's cash cow makes money one click a time. In 2016, Google's total revenue was $89.46 billion. Advertising revenue was $79.38 billion, which is 88.73% of the total revenue. Google makes majority of its money from its online advertising eco-system.

Can you explain how exactly Google makes money from its advertising ecosystem?

At a high level, Google's advertising revenue come from two group of online websites who shows Google's ads:

- Google's owned web properties such as Google's search homepage, Gmail, Map, Google Play, YouTube, etc. In 2016, Google own web properties generated $63.79 billion revenue, which account for 80% of Google advertising revenue.
- Websites Google does not own but shows Google's ads. This is commonly referred as "Google Network Members". In 2016, "Google Network Members" web sites generated $15.60 billion revenue, which account for 20% of Google advertising revenue.

Drill down to Google's Mission, Product Lineup and Business Model

Now, let's talk about Alphabet's cash cow Google -- its mission, its product lineup, how it makes money, and its implication on your interview, your Google career and your income potential.

Google's mission is to organize the world's information and make it universally accessible and useful. This is a broad and ambitious mission. It's also a mission without any mentioning of shareholder or financial metrics.

Google's core products consist of

- Search Engine
- Android
- Maps
- Chrome
- YouTube
- Google Play
- Gmail

Why are these products considered "core products"? Because each of them has over **1 billion** active users each month! Traffic and user engagement form the basis of Google's monetization. Google is a cash cow. Its economic engine starts and ends with the active users in the Google eco-system.

Let's drill down to a few important product areas.

Search: Google wasn't the first to market in search but it becomes the best search engine in the world. In late 1990s, the top search engines are Altavista, and Hotbot (created by Intokmi Corporation which was acquired by Yahoo in 2002.) Larry Page and Sergey Brin's PHD thesis formed the basis of Google's search algorithm. The founder of Inktomi was my Computer Science professor at UC Berkeley so I used to be a heavy user of Hotbot. But I remember Google just got better and better. Within a couple of years, I started to use Google exclusively.

But, in its early days Google didn't have a profitable business model. It was surviving on Venture Capital funding and losing money until it launched pay-per-click, auction based search advertising product AdWords Select. Again, this was not a new idea invented by Google. Google learned this monetization idea from Overture. But Google perfected the strategy and execution of the new Pay Per Click business model and the rest is history. I'd like to share a few observations/lessons learned:

Firstly, Google didn't invent the search engine or Pay-Per-Click advertising. But, it figured out a way to create the best search engine, and the most popular and the most profitable PPC online advertising network. Google was very good at taking something at its early stage, applying better technology to improve and scale it, and achieve massive user engagement and financial success. Later Google acquired YouTube and Android, and had great success to grow and scale both businesses. Google is great at reinvention.

Secondly, Search and AdWords revenue continue to be the major source of revenue and profit for Google. The network effect of the search business has given Google a defensible "moat", which allows Google to enjoy double digital revenue growth and a very healthy margin.

Thirdly, if you are fortunate enough to get a job at Google, I strongly encourage you to get to know the Google's search and advertising business well. Regardless of which group you are in, it's always advantageous for the employee to understand how his/her employer make money.

In addition to search and Pay-Per-Click, another product area I'd like to discuss is the creation/publishing/distribution of digital content. This is an area Google had made key acquisitions and achieved high growth.

We're all experiencing two major shifts in content consumption:

- Shift from books and DVDs to digital content
- Shift from desktop to mobile devices (e.g. mobile phones, ebook readers, etc.)

Today, we're

- Watch more videos digitally
- Play more games digitally
- Listen to more music digitally
- Read more books digitally
- Use more apps digitally

Again, Google didn't invent any of these but it has made the right investment in the entire digital content creation/publishing/distribution ecosystem:

- Platform
    - o Android
    - o Chrome Browser
    - o Chrome Operating system
- Hardware
    - o Pixel Phones
    - o Chrome Laptop
    - o Google Home
- Content
    - o Video/Music: YouTube
    - o Apps/Books/Music: Google Play Store

Who are Google's competitors?

Below is a list of major competitors in various areas. The technology market is evolving rapidly. By no means this is an all-encompassing list.

- Search engines: Microsoft Bing, Yahoo, Yandex, Baidu, Naver, Seznam
- eCommerce website: Amazon, eBay, Alibaba
- Vertical search engines:
    - o Travel vertical: Expedia, Kayak
    - o Job vertical: LinkedIn, Indeed, SimplyHired
    - o Health vertical: WebMD
- Social Network: Facebook, Twitter, Snapshot
- Online advertising network/platform: Facebook, Criteo, AppNexus
- Digital video provider: Netflix, Hulu, Amazon
- Enterprise Cloud: Amazon, Microsoft
- Digital Assistant provider: Amazon, Microsoft, Apple, Facebook
- Manufacturers of consumer electronic hardware (e.g. PC, mobile phones)

How many employees does Google have? What is the distribution by functional area?

As of December 31 2016 Google has a total of 72,053 employees.

Research & Development	27,169

Sales & Marketing	20,902
Operations	14,287
General Administration	9,695
Total	72053

Google might be too big and too slow for you

I like Google and what it stands for as a top employer. I recommend Google to most of my coaching clients. However, Google is not perfect. Like many other large company, it has its share of bureaucracy and slow decision making. If you are the entrepreneurial type who dreams about starting a company, you might get frustrated by Google's slow decision-making process and large company bureaucracy. However, Google can be beneficial to your future entrepreneurial endeavor in several ways:

- You'll work with a lot of smart and ambitious people who are the best at what they do. They can be your cofounder and future employees.
- You'll be exposed to cutting edge products and technologies that might inspire you to come up with ideas for your own venture.
- You'll gain access to Google's large and valuable alumni network. The network can help you recruit, look for investors, explore business partnerships, etc.
- People in the industry knows how rigorous Google's hiring process is. Having Google on your resume gives you credibility.
- To become such a successful company, Google has done a few things right. You might want to incorporate Google's best practices to your own company (if they are applicable).

Alphabet's "other bet" might be too risky

Outside Google's core business, some of its ventures (part of Alphabet's "other bet" portfolio) are highly speculative. They could be shut down with very little notice. If you're offered a position at one of the other ventures as part of Alphabet, you need to be careful. There might be a lot of hype and media coverage about these ventures, but some of them are very early stage.

You need carefully consider your downside: What if your project is shut down in 12 months? How will you feel if you don't create anything concrete and meaningful in 12 months? Will you still be as motivated and engaged as you're now? What is your opportunity cost?

If you are currently a middle level manager at another company and your goal is to quickly advance to senior and executive level positions, Google might not be the best place for you to reach your career goals. Most people will probably end up having same or lesser job title when moving to Google. Given its flat structure and unique managerial and leadership principles and practices, Google is not the best place for rapidly advancing one's career.

Managerial position at Google is VERY different

If you're interviewing for a manager position at Google, read this first – Google's definition of "manager" is very different.

According to Eric Schmidt, former CEO and current Executive Chairman of Google, "Managers serve the team". This means managers focuses not on punishments or rewards but on removing roadblocks and inspiring team. Google give employees a lot more trust, freedom and authority than most companies do.

Google takes power and authority over employees away from managers. Below is a sample of decisions manager at Google CANNOT make unilaterally – this is very different from any other company I have worked at:

- Hiring decision
- Firing decision
- Performance rating
- Salary increase, bonus and stock grant amount
- Promotion

Each of these decisions are made by a committee or a group of peers or a dedicated, independent team.

If you like control and authority, you will get frustrated at Google. Leadership style comes in all shapes and forms. There is no absolute right or wrong models. However, Google is looking for a leadership style that is defined by Google's unique culture. If this doesn't fit your style please do not pretend to fit in. Trying to fit a square peg into a round role don't help anyone's cause.

Google has a very strong corporate culture. Its culture has a huge impact on how it hires. It's critical for you to have a deep understanding and appreciation for Google's corporate culture before you have your first interview.

How Cofounders' background shape the culture

Both Google's cofounders (Larry and Sergey) are still heavily involved in the business today. To understand Google's culture, we need to first understand where Larry and Sergey came from and how their backgrounds had shaped the company they built.

Both Larry and Sergey were educated in the Montessori system, which gives the students a lot of freedoms to explore.

Larry's grandfather was an auto worker who carried a weapon to work to protect himself from the company. Sergey was born in the former Soviet Union, a communist regime that gave its citizens very little freedom.

They met at Stanford University's Computer Science PHD program. They enjoyed the intellectually stimulating, collegiate environment at Stanford.

Both Larry and Sergey have an anti-establishment mentality. Transparency, freedom, respect to individuals are important. They wanted to build a culture that is trusting, empowering, generous, challenging the status quo, intellectually stimulating, and collegiate. They believe in meritocracy. Fundamentally Google believes people are good.

Three Pillars of Google's culture

Missions:

Google's mission statement is to organize the world's information and make it universally accessible and useful. It didn't mention any business terms such as profit, market, customer, shareholders, or users. It's a lofty mission but an important one. Think about Sergey and his family's experience at the former Soviet Union, a dictatorship that gave its citizen very limited access to world's information. Google does the opposite. It provides freedom and access to any useful information. Anyone with an Internet connection can use Google to search for information.

Transparency:

Externally Google publishes "<u>Transparency Report</u>" that it provides visibility into data requests Google receives from the government. Internally, Google is as transparent as it can be with its employees. Every software engineer has access to almost all of Google's code base. Every employee can view the personal goals and objectives of every other employee. The company holds all-hands meetings every Thursday so that remote offices can watch a replay of the event on Friday their time.

Voice:

Google has a culture of decisions by committee to incorporate feedback from employees. The "democratic" system has resulted in some inefficiencies but it's Google's way to give every employee a voice and a real say in how the company is run.

6 Google hiring philosophy and practice

Google focuses on hiring top performers, which is defined as 90th percentile performers. The implication is that Google focuses on a very small pool of candidates – in the best-case scenario, only 10% of applicants will be top performers. This means you need to be better than 90% of the applicants.

To stay true to its goal to attract top 10% performers, Google has to take a very different approach to recruit.

Google spend more than twice as much on recruiting, as a percentage of total people budget, as an average company. Once Google hires someone, it put a lot of trust on that person and treat the person as a permanent employee who will be there for a long time. At other companies, a new hire typically has a 90-day time window to prove himself/herself. That's not the case at Google. Google invests on people upfront during the recruiting process, and fully expects the new hire will work out.

Because the hiring bar is very high and Google is unwilling to compromise, Google hires slowly. It goes through hiring committee and then senior executives for approval. The process can be frustrating to candidates.

Amazon has a bar raiser for every interview loop. The role of the bar raiser is to make sure Amazon hires people better than what they already have. Similarly, Google has an internal saying that "only hire people who are better than you". It constantly tries to get better.

In the past, you might have heard Google requesting college GPA and test scores for all positions. It was true. But, Google has changed the practice. Google used to take a more elitist approach to recruiting. It liked to hire people with pedigrees: graduates of Stanford, Harvard, MIT, UC Berkeley and Carnegie Mello and other top schools/Computer Science Programs who had also worked at the most highly regarded companies. But, Google had completely changed its position and practice. According to Laszlo Bock, Senior Vice President of people operation at Google, said in an interview with The New York Times:

"One of the things we've seen from all our data crunching is that G.P.A.'s are worthless as a criteria for hiring, and test scores are worthless. What matters is what you bring to the company and how you distinguish yourself. "

What made Google to change its mind? In 2010 Google's internal data analysis showed that academic performance didn't predict job performance beyond the first two or three years after college. As a result, Google stopped requiring grades and transcripts. The only exception is recent graduates and current students who apply for internship positions.

I was very skeptical several years ago when Google still asked candidates for their GPA and test scores. In my own career, I had worked with many "book smart" employees who were not very good employees. Some of the best employees I had never finished college or attended state schools. Academic performance is a poor indicator of job performance. I applaud Google's decision to stop asking for grades and test scores from candidates.

7 How Google makes hiring decisions?

Google's philosophy is to be objective, consistent, and minimizing cognitive biases. To carry out its hiring philosophy, Google has designed a unique system of hiring by committee.

Any hiring decision is proposed, reviewed, approved or rejected by a multi-step process:

Step 1: Hiring committee makes initial recommendation.

- review each interviewee's packet
- make the initial hire/no hire recommendation
- has zero input and visibility into compensation / offers.

Who are hiring committee?

There are hundreds of hiring committees inside Google. Each committee composed of people who were familiar with the job being filled but didn't have a direct stake in it.

For example, a hiring committee for software engineer roles would be made up of software engineers but would not include the hiring manager or anyone who would directly work with the candidate. This is to ensure objectivity.

The hiring committee include a mix of individual contributors and managers. They don't get paid; they're volunteers. And it's quite a time commitment for them to sit on the hiring committee. Each week a hiring committee member could review as many as 6-8 candidates and attend a hiring committee meeting. That can easily be 10-15 hours of work in addition to their day jobs.

Step 2: Reference Check.

Recruiter requests candidate to provide a list of external references and compensation history. Recruiter conducts the reference checks, and prepares a packet of information to be reviewed in later stages.

Step 3: Pre-Review Committee review.

These committees consist of VPs and Directors. There are limited number of Pre-Review Committees inside Google. For example, for engineering jobs, there are only 3 Pre-Review Committees globally that reviews all engineering candidate recommendations.

Step 4: Comp Review

Compensation Committee: They will determine the details of the job offers such as base pay, sign on bonus, performance bonus, and stock offers.

Step 5: SVP Review

The SVP Committee is based in Mountain View, CA. It has the ultimate decision-making power. The most common reason for rejection at this stage is Culture (value of transparency and voice).

At this point, you might think that's a lot of committees (i.e. cooks in the kitchen)! That's true. But, Google has been using this process for over a decade and it has continuously optimizing the process based on feedback and data analytics. Judging from the quality of people Google have hired over the years, it has worked well for Google. It is cleverly designed to ensure consistently high hiring bar across the company, separate hiring decision from compensation decision, minimize human cognitive biases, and apply "wisdom of crowed" to minimize hiring mistakes.

How Google recruiters source candidates?

Google has a recruiting machine. Its recruiting effort largely rely on its own internal recruiting team. To get their attention, you need to understand how Google recruiters identify potential candidates.

Google has an internal tool called gHire. It's essentially a home-grown database of candidates. Where did Google find the candidates? They come from a variety of sources:

- Internal referrals. Google values internal referrals. Referred candidates get a call within 48 hours and the referring Googler is provided weekly updates on the status of their candidates.
- LinkedIn Search: Google recruiters conduct search on LinkedIn. They generate a list of people who would be good candidate for Google.
- Hiring managers, employees, and recruiters are all part of Google's recruiting machine. For example, a hiring manager might know some very talented people from his previous employers. These people might not be available for hire. But, the hiring manager would spend years to nurture the relationship and eventually hire the person into Google.
- Google also leverage conferences and industry events to build relationships with top candidates regardless of their availability. Google is in for the long game. It is patient and relentless in its pursuit of top talents. For example, sometimes Google even uses the Internet Archive Wayback Machine to look up a candidate's old website or blogs to understand his/her history.

Action Plan to generate interest from Google

To generate interest from Google and get your first phone interview with Google, you should implement the following action plan.

1. Get to know someone at Google: Internal referral is the simple most effective way to get an interview. The key is that you need to get to know someone at Google and he/she thinks highly of your skills and experience. If you have a former colleague who works at Google, take him/her out for lunch. Pick his/her brain

about Google. Since you worked together previously, there might be opportunity for you to work together again.

2. If you don't know anyone at Google, it'll take time to build relationship with someone there. But, if you're willing to play the long game, you can wait for a year or two until you apply. You can take the time to get to know a few people at Google. You need to work hard to cultivate genuine relationships.

3. If you have opportunities to attend industry conferences that Google has a presence, I highly recommend you attend. Network with the Google employees. It'd be even better if you can submit a speaker proposal and speak at the event. It'll give you a lot of credibility and you might get Google's attention.

4. You should update your LinkedIn Profile to optimize for Google jobs. How to optimize your profile? Start with the keywords on the Google job description. Then you should search for current Google employees who hold similar job titles. Review their LinkedIn profiles. You should model your profile after theirs. Note: I'm not asking you to "copy and paste". Your profile needs to reflect your skills and experience. However, presentation and positioning of the profile can be optimized by modeling after others' profiles.

5. If you like to write and have valuable industry or technical insights to share, I highly recommend you start a blog. If you have good content that is insightful and relevant to Google, you'll get the attention of hiring managers and recruiters. The key is that you must have great insights to share. Once you have 10-15 blog posts, you can aggressively use social media channels such as Twitter and Facebook to promote your writing. Once you have enough posts, you can even turn your blog content into a self-published eBook on Amazon Kindle store. A published author adds even more credibility to your resume.

6. If you do business with Google, you are in a tricky situation. You have access to Google employees and you might even be friends with them. However, both you and your Google friends will face conflict of interest if you ask for their help to apply for a position at Google. My recommendation is to take a long view. Build and grow relationships with your Google contacts. You'll not work

for the same employer forever. Once you leave your current employer, you'll be free to ask your Google contacts to help you. Cultivate the relationship now, and you will benefit down the road.

7. Contribute to open source projects: Contribute to open source projects. Make your codes available on GitHub. Build something useful. You'll get Google's attention.

Google Career Website: This is where you submit your application. Unlike most other company career websites, Google has an excellent career website. Please spend time to read every section of the career website. Search for openings. Create your application and submit. Your Google application will use your Google login. If you have multiple Google logins, please be careful which login you use because Google will have access to your social media footprint (e.g. Google Plus.)

Google's internal reference checking system

Google checks a job applicant's resume against the resumes of existing Google employees. If there is a relationship (e.g. the job applicants attended the same college as a Googler, or worked at a previous employer at the same time), the Google employee will often receive an email asking their opinion of the job applicant. This information is incorporated into a hiring packet of 50 pages or more per candidate and reviewed by the hiring committee. Google values opinions of its employees. If you know current Google employees who can speak highly of your skills and experience, please reach out to them for referral and recommendation.

Should you work with 3rd party recruiters?

For most positions, the answer is "no". Google does NOT have a good history to work with 3rd-party recruiters.

Google prefers contingency search fees arrangement over retainer's fees. This means recruiter only gets paid if a candidate is successfully hired. However, Google has extremely high bar for hiring, and the acceptance rate is very low. This means 3rd-party recruiters have to work really hard, go through many candidates before they can finally have someone getting hired by Google and got paid.

There are exceptions. If you work in a non-US market that Google doesn't have a strong hold, Google might use 3rd party recruiters to help find the right candidates. Also, for certain senior level positions, Google might seek the help of top search firms to identify and connect with the right candidates.

9 What types of interview questions should you expect?

I'll provide you a list of sample interview questions with tips. But, before I give you the list of questions, it's important to understand from Google's perspective what type of questions best predict how well a candidate will perform in a job.

According to Google, the best predictor of how someone will perform in a job is a work sample test. This entails giving candidates a sample piece of work, like what they would do in the job, and assessing their performance at it.

The second-best predictor of performance are tests of general cognitive ability. These are not case interviews and brainteasers with open-ended answers. These are actual test with definitive right and wrong answers. smart people who can learn and adapt to new situation. This is about understanding how candidates have solved hard problems in real life and how they learn, not checking GPAs and SATs.

Brainteaser questions: In the past Google had a reputation for asking brainteaser questions. Their internal data had shown that brainteaser questions are poor predictor of employees' future success inside Google. So, officially Google discourage brain teasers. But, sometimes interviewers still do ask this type of questions. When senior leaders review applicants each week, they ignore the answers to brain teaser questions. So, you might still encounter brain teaser questions but you will not be rejected because you didn't do well in answering brainteaser questions.

The third best predictor are structured interviews, where candidates are asked a consistent set of questions with clear criteria to assess the quality of responses. The structured questions allow the various committees to assess applicants with a consistent set of criteria. Google has a database off "canned questions" for interviewers to choose.

Google has a strong culture and it takes its culture seriously. It is looking for people who fit into their culture. You could ace all your technical interviews but still not getting a job offer because Google doesn't feel you are a good culture fit. This is absolutely a critical area of your interview process.

Below is a list of key components of Google culture.

Intellectual humility

Google interviewers value humility. They don't like arrogant people who lack self-awareness. You might think that it's easy to "fake" humility. As a hiring manager in several companies, I can tell you that "intellectual humility" cannot be faked. In fact, over the years, I have interviewed so many candidates who lacked humility and self-awareness that I now include "humility and self-awareness" in every single job description I write. If you wonder what exactly are "humility and self-awareness", let me give you my definition:

- You are aware of what you know and what you don't know.
- You know your limitations.
- You try to avoid "when I have a hammer, every problem is a nail" cognitive bias.
- You're an excellent listener. You seek to listen and understand instead of focusing on showing off to the world how much you know.
- You're intellectually curious and you're a learning machine.

Instead of focusing on showing the world how much you know and how great you are, it's much more fun, interesting and productive to be a learning machine. A great role model is Warren Buffet, who is a better investor today at age 86 than he had ever been because he is constantly learning.

Conscientiousness

This is a big word. What exactly does "conscientiousness" mean in this context? Google wants employees who has an ownership mentality instead of employee mentality.

People with employee mentality is task oriented. They focus on getting the tasks completed so that they can collect the paycheck. People with ownership mentality are different. They treat the company as their own business. They truly care about the success of the business. It's not just a job for them. They care about the company's mission. They seek to understand business strategy. They monitor the company performance. They are constantly looking for ways to improve the business. They are actively engaged in the company day-to-day operation.

Comfort level and ability to deal with ambiguity

Google operates in a highly dynamic environment. It is competing in many new areas that is evolving quickly. You must be able to deal with ambiguities. If you're not given a clear direction, are you capable of taking the initiative to define a problem statement and figuring out a solution on your own? The ability to put a structure around a problem and figure out a solution is extremely valuable. Additionally, Google is a large company. It has a flat structure. You'll need to navigate the organization to get things done. Nobody is going to hold your hands to navigate the organization. You need to be able to find your way inside Google. This is another aspect of dealing with ambiguities.

Evidence you have taken some courageous or interesting paths in your life

Google wants to get to know you during the interview process. Please do not make up a story to differentiate yourself. Everyone is unique. Everyone has a story to tell. The key is for you to search deep inside, and identify the unique life story/life path you have taken.

Enjoy and have fun

We all want to work with people who are enthusiastic and enjoy what they do.

Role related knowledge

This is what we normally call "domain knowledge". By far this is the least important attribute to Google. Google's perspective is someone who has done the same task successfully for many years is likely to see a situation at Google and replicate the same solution that has worked for them. "Once you have a hammer, every problem is a nail". Google is looking for people who will think creatively and figure out new approaches to solve a problem. Google's core DNA is "re-invention". However, I do want to say that this has changed a little bit in recent years. Google is a very large company now. Its business has also matured. Instead of being the upstart disrupter, Google is now the target for disruption. With the established and well run existing business models, it makes more sense for Google to hire people who has some or deeper domain knowledge. So, role related knowledge is getting more important for the interview process as Google evolves.

Leadership

Google looks for a particular type of leaders, called "emergent leadership". Below is a list of characteristics of "emergent leadership":

- Care less about formal designation/job titles – if you're on a corporate fast track and want to get bigger titles quickly, Google is probably not the right company for you.
- Everyone can be a leader when you have the right skills to solve a business problem. Google expects that over a team's life different skills will be needed at different times, so various people will need to step into leadership roles, contribute, and step back once the need for their specific skills has passed. Everyone needs to learn to lead and follow. This reminds me a key lesson I learned at an MBA leadership class. My professor, who was a very successful executive in his previous life, told us that a great leader is a great follower first.
- Google has a strong bias against leaders who are about themselves. These are people who use "I" far more than "we". They focus on promoting themselves internally and what they have accomplished.

11 Google Interview Process Walk Through

I'll walk you through the interview process from initial phone screen to onsite interviews. Before I do that I'd like to address a few frequently asked questions.

Who will be your interviewers?

- Perspective manager (where possible – for some large job groups like "software engineer" or "Account strategist" there is no single hiring manager)
- Peers
- One or two of the people who will work for you (if you apply for managerial positions).
- Cross functional interviewer: someone with little or no connection at all to the group for which the candidate is interviewing. This person has no interests in the particular job filled but has a strong interest in keeping the quality of hiring high. This is almost like the bar raiser concept in Amazon.

How many people you'll be talking to?

Google used to have candidates to talk to a lot of interviewers but it was very time consuming and inefficient. Google analyzed its hiring data, and came up with "rule of 4", which limits the number of interviews a candidate could have onsite to about 4 people. They do allow exceptions in certain cases. Google's internal analytics showed that 4 onsite interviews were enough to predict whether or not Google should hire someone with 86 percent confidence. Based on our own client feedback, you should expect an average of 5 interviews so Google hasn't strictly followed it "rule of 4".

Why Google interviewers tend to take copious amount of notes during interview?

They are required to write down

- the attributes being assessed
- the question asked
- the candidate's answer
- the interviewer's assessment of the answer

So please do not be offended or disturbed by the interviewer's lack of eye contact and/or endless typing.

Phone/Hangout Interview

During phone or Google Hangout interviews, you'll speak with a potential peer or manager. Normally you will have 2 phone screens. We have heard in some cases a candidate only has one phone interview before having onsite interviews.

For software engineering roles, your phone/Hangout discussion will last about 45 minutes. You phone interview will cover data structures and algorithms. You should be prepared to write code in your strongest programming language. When answering coding questions, make sure you ask clarifying question. Yu should talk through your thought process. It's important for the interviewer to understand your thought process. Also, you don't want to misunderstand the question – you'll waste a lot of time if you write codes to solve the wrong problem! You should use a hands-free headset or speakerphone so you can type freely on Google Doc.

You should write workable code. Don't try to write the perfect code as your time is limited. Once you finish writing the code, you should also think about how to optimize the code, follow it with test cases, and find any bugs.

 If you're interviewing for non-technical positions, your phone/Hangout discussion will last between 30 and 45 minutes. Be prepared for behavioral, hypothetical, or case-based questions that cover your role-related knowledge.

Onsite Interview

For your onsite interview loop, you will meet between 4 and 6 people. Most people seem to have 4-5 interviewers. Some of them are your peers while others are cross functional stakeholders who might work with you. Each interview will be 30-45 minutes long. As I described earlier, you should expect questions that test your general cognitive ability, your technical skills (for technical positions), leadership skills, role related knowledge, and culture fit (i.e. Googleyness).

12 Capstone: How to Emulate Google Employee to Ace Interviews

This is the most unique section of this book. Google is a unique company with a very different recruiting and hiring approach. I have shared a lot of inside details about Google. But, I feel that I need to give you more specific examples to help you understand what kind of people do well in Google. If you model after these people, you'll dramatically increase your chance to succeed.

Fortunately, I worked in online advertising for over a decade. My career coincided with Google's rise in Google Advertising. I had worked with people from multiple functional areas inside Google, including client services, ad operation, sales, marketing, partnership, education, product management and engineering. Additionally, in the early 2000s, several of my engineering colleagues at a Silicon Valley start-up joined Google as early employees. I got a good sense of who're the great engineers Google had hired in its early days. These engineers formed the early foundation of Google, and helped shaped the culture.

In this section, I'll share with you my experience of working with various folks at Google, what made them great, and how you should model after them as you prepare for your interview.

Before I start, let me share with you an inspirational quote:

"The surest way to achieve success is to model someone who is already successful. If you don't have good models, find someone who is the best in your chosen field and emulate them. You don't need to reinvent the wheel – simply learn from the best." – Tony Robbins

I initially learned about the power of Google in 2004 when I started working at Amazon. At that time, Amazon stock price was trading at $34 per share as it just recovered from the dot come crash. I was working for a team that was responsible for generating traffic to Amazon.com. I remembered my boss put together a business review document to present to the senior management team. The title of the presentation was "The House is On Fire". You never wanted your own house to be on fire, so the presentation caught my attention.

Apparently, Google was driving so much traffic to Amazon that it's essentially serving as a huge "traffic distributor" to Amazon. Amazon was very concerned about the leverage Google would have if it continued its exponential growth.

Google was growing so fast because it had three things going for it:

1. It re-invented how online search was done, and it was absolutely the best search engine in the world. There is also a self-reinforcing cycle here – the more users Google had, the more data points Google had to improve its search results which in turn attracted more users.
2. Google's Ad Words product was taking off. It was responsible for driving a lot of traffic to retailer web sites. The paid ads cost retailers a lot of money but they really worked.
3. Google's organic search results continue to drive a lot of traffic to retailer websites as well.

Over the past decade, Google has continued to improve in the 3 areas, which continue to be the most important foundation of Google's business model.

How was Google able to "re-invent" and build such great products? Let me share with you what I know about Google engineers and Product Managers. This will also explain what Google is looking for during the interview process.

The early engineers I know are "hard core" engineers. They studied Computer Science at top programs such as Stanford, Berkeley, MIT, CMU, etc. There was also exception as some people never finished college. However, they shared a few common traits:

• They have a passion for technology. They didn't choose Computer Science because it would get them high paying jobs. They really enjoyed Computer Science.

• A lot of them started programming early.

• They take a lot of pride in their work. They love solving hard problems.

• They have a strong foundation in algorithm and data structure. As I mentioned, Google is about reinvention. To be better than everyone else in search and other areas, the engineers must figure out the best, and most optimal solution. You won't be able to code your way to success. You need a strong theoretical foundation. That's where a strong foundation in algorithm and data structure come to play.

- They believe in meritocracy -- "the best idea wins". There is no room for BS. If you don't know something, admit it.
- Some of them might sound or look a little bit arrogant because they're very smart. But, if you get to know them, you'd appreciate their brilliance.
- As they "reinvent" solutions to hard problems, they have to think methodically, creatively, and critically. There is no existing blueprint to follow. They are excellent thinkers – this is why General Cognitive Ability is a very important part of Google interview process. They want to hire people who know how to think.

Many of above characteristics have been embedded into Google culture. For example, if you are interviewing for a technical position at Google, you need to brush up your algorithm and data structure knowledge.

As an online marketer, I have been working with Google advertising ecosystem for the past decade. I used to manage a large e-commerce business in the Health & Wellness category. I managed a marketing spend of $10M+ annually. About half of these budgets were spent with Google Ad Words. This was a super competitive niche. A click on Google would cost me $7 or more. To acquire a new customer, I had to pay over $40 per order. This is when I came to appreciate the cash cow called Google! Whenever someone clicks on an ad I won on Google auction, Google made $7 or more! It's a highly scalable business model with almost zero margin cost to Google.

Our marketing spend was large enough that I would have quarterly and annual meeting with Google's account team. So, I had plenty of interactions with Google's account management team and ad operation team. I was constantly impressed by the caliber of Google people. They were much better than other ad companies. Below is a list of what I appreciated about Google's account management and ad ops team.

They are smart and they can think. Sometimes I would see abnormal increase in cost per order. The change was so dramatic that I really needed an explanation. This required someone on Google's side dive deep into data and use data to explain what happened. When I had similar problem with other ad companies, their account managers would give me an "intuitive answer" (i.e. they think "x, y, z" happened.) But their answers were speculative without a logical thought process. Google's account team would explain to me in a step by step fashion. For example, ad performance boiled down to several key metrics such as impression share, number of impressions, click through rate, conversion, etc. Google's team was always able to walk me through the entire conversion funnel, use data to explain what happened, and reach a logical conclusion that was conclusive. This example is a reflection of Google's emphasis in evaluating candidate's general cognitive ability. You need to have a structured way to solve problems. You need to be able to break problem down into parts, and divide and conquer. Use data to inform you decision and use data to validate assumptions. Reach logical conclusion.

Google folks are authentic, genuine and nice. There are always exceptions. But, for the most parts, the Google employees I worked with were good and nice people. They were very responsive. They always returned emails or phone calls on a timely fashion. They were polished in their communication and delivery. They were also very good at dealing with organizational ambiguities. For example, I once worked for a company that went through several re-orgs. The Google account team was very good at dealing with the org change. They proactively reached out to the new leaders, and immediately set up weekly/monthly/quarterly meetings. It's very easy for external vendors to get lost in the organization shuffles of a client organization. But, it never happened with the Google team. They're very proactive in dealing with ambiguities and uncertainties. They built relationships and knew a great deal about their clients' business and organization. The ability to deal with ambiguities is a key attribute for evaluation during the interview process. You should think about stories from you past work history that demonstrate how you put a structure around an ambiguous situation, and proactively bring clarity and solution to the situation.

I also had the opportunities to provide product feedback to Google's product management team. It was a very interesting experience to visit Google's executive briefing center in Mountain View, CA. Here is what I learned from my experience to interact with Google's product management leaders.

Google has a very flat structure. Someone with the job title "Product Manager" or "Group Product Manager" could be given significant amount of responsibilities. Some of them had VP or Director job titles at their previous jobs but they were happy to have the "PM" or "GPM" job titles at Google.

They were very smart people who really knew their subject area. However, if you career goal is to move up quickly in corporate ladder with higher job titles, I think you should think twice before you apply for Google jobs. It's not a place for getting bigger job titles. That's not Google's culture.

Google's PM team is very end user focused. As a major advertiser, I expressed my concerns about certain Google features that forced me to pay more that resulted in higher advertising spend. Google's PM's response started with end user impact – if it is something that benefits the end consumer, Google will continue to do it. This is very similar to Amazon's approach of "start with customer and work backward".

Google's PM team is very analytical and data driven. When I challenged Google team about certain product decision they had made, the PM immediately shared with me what A/B tests had been done, and how they came to the decision. It was very clear that they made the decision based in quantitative data. When Google recruiter talks about General Cognitive Ability, they meant the ability to think critically, and use data to make informed decisions.

Behavioral Interview Tip

Google takes its culture very seriously and culture fit is a critical factor in the hiring process. In addition to practice sample interview questions, I'd like to recommend you take the following steps:

1. Careful read the job description
2. Make a bullet list of key attributes in the job description that Google is looking for
3. For each attribute, prepare 1-3 examples/stories related to the attribute
4. Write down your examples and practice them verbally

You should do this exercise in addition to practice sample questions

Sample Behavioral Questions

- Why Google?
- Why do you want this job?
- What does "being Googley" mean to you?
- Tell me about a time your behavior had a positive impact on your team. What was your primary goal and why? How did your teammates respond? Moving forward, what is your plan?
- Tell me about a time when you effectively managed your team to achieve a goal. What did your approach look like? What were your targets and how did you meet them as an individual and as a team? How did you adapt your leadership approach to different individuals? What was the key takeaway from this specific situation
- Tell me about a time you had difficulty working with someone (can be a coworker, classmate, client). What made this person difficult to work with for you? What steps did you take to resolve the problem? What was the outcome? What could you have done differently?)
- Describe one of the difficulties you have encountered.
- "Tell me about two suggestions you have made to your manager in the past year. How did you come up with the ideas? What happened? How do you feel about the way things went?"
- "Describe a situation where you were responsible for getting others

to make a change. What role did you play and what actions did you take? What was the outcome? If you had to do it again, would you do anything differently?"
- "How does the work you are currently doing affect your organization's ability to meet its mission and goals? Do you think your work is important? If yes, why? If no, why not?"
- What would you want to do if you didn't have to work?
- If you could be remembered for one sentence, what would it be?
- If you could only choose one song to play every time you walked into a room for the rest of your life, what would it be?
- What three things would you change at your university/workplace if you were CEO today?
- Tell me something about you that isn't on your résumé.
- If I gave you $10 million right now, what would you do?

Technical Interview Tips

- It's very important for you to explain clearly your thought process and decision making. Google evaluates not only your technical capabilities but also how you solve problems.
- If you're making assumptions, make sure you clearly state the assumptions. You should also assess if the assumption is reasonable. Talk through your thought process with the interviewer.
- If a question doesn't sound very clear to you, you should ask clarifying questions. Trust your intuition. If something is not clear, it's probably not clear. The worst thing is for you to spend 30 minutes to work on the wrong problem.
- When you finish coding, think about how you would test and optimize. These are key attributes you should demonstrate during interview.
- For coding questions, you're expected to write detailed codes, check input, and handle special cases. You might also be asked to provide time/space complexity.
- Algorithm: you should refresh your algorithm knowledge. Here is a list of common algorithms that you might need for Google interviews
    o   Sorting
    o   Recursion
    o   Divide and Conquer

- o Dynamic Programming
  - o You should know Big O notation
  - o You should which algorithms tend to go with what data structure
- Data structures:
  - o Arrays
  - o Linked List
  - o Stacks
  - o Queues
  - o Hash-sets
  - o Hash-maps
  - o Hash-table
  - o Dictionary
  - o Trees
  - o Binary Trees
  - o Heaps
  - o Graphs

Technical Interview Sample Questions

- What you know about HashTable? Benefits.
- When you debug a Java program, you insert a System.out.print to output the debug, but you found the debug is gone. Any reason?
- Image a sorted array 1,2,3,8,10,20,49. After a shift happens, for example, it happens at 10. All elements including and after 10 are pasted in the beginning. The array becomes 10,20,49,1,2,3,8. Now ask to find an element (say, 3). What is your best solution?
- Write a function to return the largest two integers in an array.
- Write a function to implement a buffer for DataOutputStream. How are you going to test it?
- Write a function to determine whether a word is in a dictionary. How will you test it?
- Implement a code to do wildcard string matching (e.g. source: readme.txt, query: *.txt, should return true.)
- Check whether a Sudoku is valid. 9*9 matrix, and each row, column and 3*3
cell only contain unique integers (in range [1,9]) or empty

- Find intersection of two sorted array A, B
- Check whether a binary tree is a binary search tree
- Sampling of incoming integers, then return one sample with equal probability.   The major advantages and disadvantages of following languages: C++, Python, Java. (He asked for at least 3 disadvantages for each language, if you can only give two, he will continue to let you think)..
- Consider you are constructing a system for data synchronization, what problem will you face, and how you solve it?
- What is mutex, semaphore, deadlock? Give examples of them.
- A string consists of '0', '1' and '?'. The question mark can be either '0' or '1'. Find all possible combinations for a string.
- Give you a text file, remove duplicated lines.
- Find the peak in given array.
- How to determine whether number is power of 2 or not
- Find n closest points to the origin

Google Statistician Interview Sample Questions

- How to generate random number in R
- Senior high school students go to see college admission committee (10 members totally). Each committee member will give a result for the candidate: accepted/rejected/waiting list. 1 year later, we would have how those students doing at college. Question: how can we determine whether the committee was doing a good job or not/or how can we determine whether each member was doing a good job or not
- Questions related to logistic regression model: Given an example you have built -- how to select variable, how to do validation, how to use it, how to improve it.
- There are 5 toys at KFC, and if you go there, you will get one toy totally randomly. How many times you need to go to KFC in order to get all 5 toys.

Google Product Management Sample Questions

- What are 7 ways to estimate the size of the global fishing industry.
- What is your favorite Google product? What do you like/dislike about it? How would you improve?

- How would you improve Gmail?
- How would you improve Google Map?
- How would you reduce Google Drive's storage size?
- If you can recommend Google to build one killer new feature, what would it be?
- How many Android Phones are sold in the United States in a year?
- You're the PM for Gmail. What metrics will you use to measure success of the products?
- You have a grocery delivery service (similar to Amazon Fresh) that delivers food within 24 hours. Estimate how many trucks you need to operate this service.
- How would you explain cloud computing to a 6-year-old?
- If you're the CEO of Google, will you be concerned about Amazon?
- What is the market for driverless cars in the year 2020?
- You have a colony on Mars that you want to communicate with. How do you build a system to communicate with them?
- If you had access to a bank's database, how would you use that information to design an ATM for elderly people?
- Design a mobile social app for a chain of local orthodontist offices
- What is the number of new book titles published in the U.S. each year?

Google Account Strategist Sample Interview Questions

- If ads were removed from YouTube, how would you monetize it?
- If you wanted to bring your dog to work but one of your team members was allergic to dogs, what would you do?
- Which do you think has more advertising potential in Boston, a flower shop or a funeral home?
- Describe AdWords to a 7-year-old.

14 Final Thoughts and Action Plan

I want to share with you a checklist of actions for you to take in the next few days to get ready for your Google interview:

1. Read this entire book.
2. No matter which position you're applying for, you must demonstrate your Googleyness. If you have time to re-read one thing, that'll be chapter 10.
3. Review the job description, and make a list of key attributes they're looking for. For each attribute, prepare 1-3 examples. This is a very effective way to prepare for behavioral interview questions.
4. Practice as many questions as possible and selectively read recommended books and articles. You can download a list of additional resources at http://www.nailyourjobinterview.com/google-list/.
5. If you want 1-on-1 coaching and interview practice, you can sign up at http://www.nailyourjobinterview.com/coaching/

www.ingramcontent.com/pod-product-compliance
Lightning Source LLC
Chambersburg PA
CBHW030416160726
47992CB00007B/3149